The metal of a gun

Index

Dedication

Once again, to my fabulous family, who support my weird and wonderful ways.
Specifically my mum, for proofreading everything for me with such care - the same in which she provides us with.
To my love, who is still my biggest inspiration.
To Mrs. J. Gerlach, who is always a delight to talk to.
To Mr. M. Phillips, who taught by example that it is okay to be ever so slightly insane.
And to the friends we're yet to make.

Atlantis to orbit

The gentle feathers beneath your resting head,
Holding a thousand dreams.
Your pillow like a camera,
Capturing portraits of your emotions.
Whispering softly,
the sound of waves and rain,
The sound of silence and pain.
Your aura spills,
A pallet of colours flying everywhere.
Shades of blue,
being the most frequent.
Your heavy head holds no weight,
Solely discussions of 'what if's.

Bitter-sweet

There's nothing,
like the feeling of holding a cup of coffee.
Hugging the mug with your smitten mitten hands,
Carefully lifting the addictive magma.
Slicken lavafall oiling your buds,
The swallowing of cloud like satin.
If i'd never felt warm enough,
Especially within myself.
I've justified a morning sickness,
To feel a sense of not wanting to depart from bed.
Nothing starts my morning like a cup of coffee,
Without the inviting swallow I would be merely a day.
The bitter taste left on my tongue,
Doing nothing but taunting the next sweet sip.

Water to wine

I jump,
The river surrounding me,
So much more prolific in life,
This feeling.
I was never one to be able to swim,
But I didn't assume that would give me life,
Give me a reason to live.
For let's be honest,
The true reason to live is that you get to die.
Death inches closer,
The knot around your neck getting tighter,
Breathe - more desperate than ever.
Have you ever been in an ocean during a storm?
God it's life inspiring,
Possibility breaking,
Crashing before you.
Getting drenched,
more so than before,
More so than you imagined possible.
Water in all forms hydrating your skin,
Seeping into your lungs.
The water hugs me,
Feels like a friend,
One that talks behind my back.
The water comforts me,
Like a lover,
I let it fill me all the same.

The right kind of wrong

Your lips taste like fireworks,
Your body like butterflies.
Your thoughts taste like sugar,
They also taste of lies.

Your touch feels like poison,
The right kind of wrong.
Your words sound like a lullaby,
Abusing the melody of a stupid break-up song.

Your pain feels like air,
Whilst mine feels like fire.
You've made me your own, my master,
I serve your every stinging desire.

Bump

I see you everywhere I go,
In every unique path.
You make me feel so lost my dear,
You fill me with such wrath.

I follow you swiftly,
In my dreams,
As you are always there.
But soon you're gone,
Like a burnt out star,
And I'm left to feel so bare.

I catch up to you,
As I catch my breath,
I go to kiss your lips of wine -
But I walk into a mirror instead,
And it seems I've lost my time.

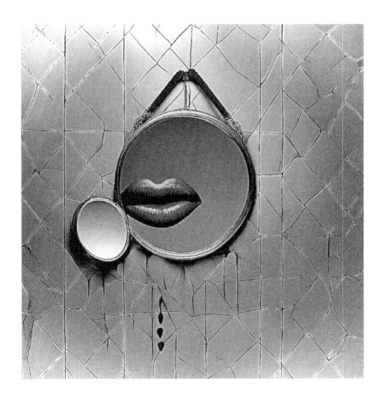

Banshee

Wailing rivers,
Sorrowful moats,
around castles built of lies.
Must I remember?
Reflect upon a ghost,
A spirit lies unspoken,
Or maybe simply unheard.
I ask you for nothing,
And I receive it in abundance.
The blood spilled for you,
Willing or nay,
Could douse a thousand white flags.
Whose hands killed the people?
Does it truly matter,
For its under your pretences,
Whether false or pure.
Haunted by loss,
Dragged to hell by the dead,
Tucked into a grave of contamination.
Run from your problems,
Or face them with a dagger of death's kiss.
Hide from the Satan ruled over world,
Keep sane inside insanity.

So close yet so far

You shine golden, like a star,
Your hot touch marks a scar.
My skin, left boundless char,
So close, yet so far.

A gloomy door ajar,
Inside keeps my inky heart.
Suffocating in love made of tar,
So close, yet so far.

My expectations raise the bar,
Your love grows eternal roses,
Thanks to your light in the dark,
And the water spilled from love.
So close, yet so far.

Desperate pits I find myself in,
Doors away from you, locked.
Keys in the hands of God, lost,
I'll never reach your desires.
So close, yet so far.

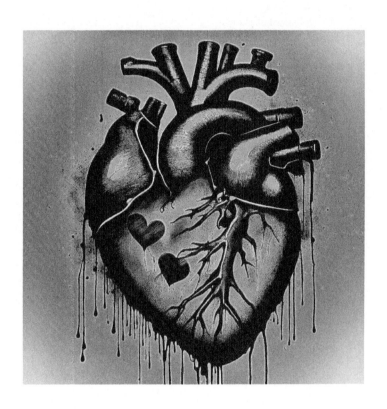

A&E acquaintances

'The current waiting time is 6 hours',
Displayed in a bleeding attention grabbing red.
If you could take a seat for me?
And so it begins,
The wait of a lifetime,
The wait for a life.

3 empty seats,
All spread apart.
One next to a woman who looks like a dormouse,
One half taken by a mother and a child,
sleeping on her lap with her feet stretched further than her hope of
getting out of here.

The last by a man,
Serious as ever.
Overwhelming his eerie stolen face full of wrinkles,
Each line signifying a year of his life.
Like an old oak,
With as many stories to tell.

The mood low,
Why wouldn't it be?
All faces blank of emotion,
Yet all mouths tell stories to one another.
Within the first hour of six,
Knowing as much as their mother would.

Within the next two,
Fetching a meal.
Made of kindness and pleasure of a friend,
Joy for someone to talk to after so long.
The waiting room erupting in cheers,
Every time a person is called through.
Funny, considering the reasons they may be here,
Are we cheering as they get to find out how long they have left to share
their stories.

The two hours after that,
The room changing significantly.
The old oak and his companion,
Boring each other to death with words,
Lucky this is a hospital.

'Great Oak' flashes in red on the same screen hours later,
Six to be exact.
The pal on his shoulder asleep,
He didn't want to leave his friend,
The one that cared.

He wakes his link,
Tells him he has to go in,
But instead, he went up.
The friend,
The sapling that gained all the knowledge of the old oak.
He'd earned his rings,
And wore them with pride.
Remembering the truly great man,
Who inspired life into him,
After giving his.

Unity

*U*nderstand, that it's not you, it's time.
*N*ever think they are your problems, because they're mine.
I shout, that our love is not at all thrown.
*T*rust that I just need some time alone.
*Y*earn for me, Time fated and thrown, mine and my dreaded notions, alone.

Wreck

I sit and I watch,
For the fly to fall for the trap.
To land in the sun's glass,
And for the lamp to fall -
Making fragments of the marble floor.

The blue ribbon comes undone,
And the pennies on the wall are falling.
Your copper hair,
I wrap around my finger,
And pray for the clouds to turn to water.

As we bend wooden promises,
To make our overlooked world,
I sense a change,
In the flow of the river.
The wires fall fast to our feet.

There's a towel on the water,
And there's water on the ground,
Oh, why do we age so quickly?

Innocent until proven guilty

Call me what you want,
Just don't blame me for a crime I didn't commit.
Your so thought poisonous words,
are extremely empowering to me.

I love when you cat call me,
I'll never respond.
So your masculinity shrivels,
Causing you to need to spit your venom at me,
To feel a speck of safety in your sadness.

As soon as I hear your shouts,
That to me sound more like cries,
A grin emerges,
Stretching to my sun lit cheeks.
I feed on your toxic words,
As if there's nothing else that could nourish me.

When you call me "faggot",
I'm proud of myself,
for being brave enough to earn that title.
So I like wearing skirts?
You call me "tranny",
I'll always embrace it.

You may be able to knock me down with your hands,
I'll never give you the chance to do so with your words.
When you call me a name,
I feel prideful,
Bathe in the fact I've built something of myself with a foundation of ego.

I ask you,
What have you done to earn such pleasure?

Le vin rouge

I chose the red,
For the sound it makes,
When it hits the bottom of the glass.

For the silk,
washing over my ivories,
Striking pain and tempting a laugh.

Licking my buds,
Escaping under my tongue,
A crash, tasting rich and bold.

I think of your lips,
How it would feel in your mouth,
My warm breath, suddenly drawn cold.

I'll always choose red,
As the oil to my words,
The remedy to my thoughts of blue.

I'm now done with my mind,
And done with my words,
I wish I could be done with you.

Uncomfortable loving

I could make you melt,
With my silver tongue,
And a strike of my belt.

You would feel my love,
The rage that gave it life,
The escape of a magician's dove.

It's always been your words taunting me,
I could persuade that same lust,
As you take every pure thing you see.

I will haunt your worst dreams,
The best nightmares,
I'll feed on your well earned screams.

I never strived to hurt you,
But surely it's fair,
Considering the scars you've left blue.

Royal decree

Kneel for me,
And on thy way up,
Scrape thy knee.

Cry for me,
Pour me a river,
Nay, a sea.

Bow for me,
I be thy king,
Nay lover nor trustee.

Live for me,
Thee bleeds over everything,
As far as the eye can see.

Die for me,
As so to restore,
The great monarchy.

Pray for me,
The devil's queen,
The crown flees.

Gasp for air

Love a cloud
In its grace and it's prime,
Trust the cloud,
Revealing itself in all soft shapes.

Climb atop it,
It promises you -
"The sky is the limit",
Trust the cloud.
And the cloud fulfilled its word,
Silly me,
As clouds don't speak.

Come,
Guide my winds,
Glide with me,
you soft gust.
Go,
Bring rope and a blanket,
I'll bring you further than the skies.
We'll shoot for the moon,
And be sure to land amongst the stars.

So the little light came,
With rope, a blanket and hope.
Tie the rope on my head,
And around yours.
Trust the cloud,
It will carry you through storms.

Love a cloud,
Lifted above all else as vowed.
The light now a plank,
The plank now a swing.
Gifted with marks,
Scars from the palest cloud of all.

Trust the cloud,
You're above all heavens,
Let the forest ball.
You may hang,
Little stone plank,
But rely,
You'll never fall.

Untitled

I don't care for tomorrow,
I don't care for to day,
Nor do I for the past -
I couldn't care either way.

To give you something
Anything at all,
One little drop of care,
Would barely ever happen
Oh it would be quite rare.

For apathy is the eighth sin,
And energy is strength.
No effort is given around me,
So why on earth go to such a length.

Egg

Throw me against a wall,
Let me fall to the floor,
My body running down the surface like a yolk,

Yet I'm never broken.

Stab me with your words,
Kill me with a sentence,
I still won't break a crack.

Love me like a devil,
Soothe and groom me,
Give me your heart,
Sunny side up.

Throw me against a wall,
Let my body fall to the floor,
My body running down the surface like a yolk,

You've broken my heart,

Therefore - my shell cracks.

Full and yellow,
A yolk,
Pure and white,
Scrambled.

Hate

I hate loving him,
I hate him so fucking much.
I hate every breath he takes,
And every breath he doesn't.

I hate that he can't choose to love me or hate me,
I'd rather him feel the same.

I hate the ground he walks on,
I hate that I can't follow in his footsteps to dig them up with my heels.

I hate that hate isn't nearly strong enough,
It comes nowhere near to the strength of my heart.
The pathetic passion of hate.

The fall

The fail of the fall,
is the worst part of all,
The guts to spill guts,
and the nerve to kill nerves.
It takes and it takes,
Til' it's tempted to serve.

The want for the fall,
Is the worst part of all,
The light in your heart,
Plastered then ripped apart.
The thoughts held to much,
So you drop it from the clutch.

The thrive of the fall,
Is the worst part of all,
The adrenaline rush,
The release of deaths hush.
The want for succession,
Via murder of depression.

The president's green thumb

The president's green thumb,
Wasn't one of plants or leaves.
But money by the paper load,
A greedy need for green.

Civilians found it offensive,
More for the powerful son.
No chance for our future,
Just theories of the triangle with one.

Our grandmothers cry,
For us to live like them.
Not in a chair that rocks,
But for our nurture,
A delicate mother hen.

The manage of the overseer,
With his blade of gold to our throat.
The elevator taking him,
High above our moat.
When it should be going down,
A sacrifice of a greed filled goat.

"Dear, my valentines"

We share our woeful love,
Dish out desire by the dozen.
Cover the bed in petals of blood,
Hang your heart up on the ceiling.

The one day a year,
I can truly be transparent.
When it's socially acceptable,
To lay my beating organ bare.

Partners of a lifetime,
Rushing to buy last minute trinkets.
When I planned this a lifetime ago,
The desperation to get to be in love.

"Dear, my valentines",
I've ruined me, for you.
I've stabbed myself with a poison dagger,
As I will continue to do.

Literary legends

To copy the words of shakespeare,
Urge to live with his fame.
To be mentioned in the same breath,
As "A rose by any other name".

To be as creative as Dr.seuss,
Though never to compare.
Thrive to be "Youer than you",
Aware of the rare that is there.

To brave the 'It' of a king,
To fail is to embrace the shining.
Carrie the weight on your back,
Shed blood, spill tears, enshrining.

To write the thoughts of a great detective,
Deaths on boats and trains alike.
Travelling extravagant mysteries,
Where will the next murderer strike?

To twist your mind like de sade,
Write the harshest of tales for the time.
Go insane with literary genius,
Love is truly a crime.

Shorts

The sex appeal of shorts,
I have never given thought.
But with nothing much to worry on,
I truly have been taught.

Leather, jean or tailored silk,
Tis' really quite a taste,
For when you wear your fitting shorts,
Your ass hath not gone to waste.

Oh boy, oh dear,
My one love's shorts,
That for them she's grown too big.
The excitement gets a hold of me,
And I fall prey to an endless jig.

Beautiful beast

A kiss is all I could ask of you,
But I'm restrained from thinking to try.
If I did steal one finally, I'd get a taste for all I couldn't have,
I would suck the blood from them, draining you of wondering love.

I just want to be covered in you,
A blanket of warmth of your touch.
The drama in longing for someone forbid,
Like accepting a rose by its thorns.

You coward, run away from me all you want,
I'll always leave my fragrance.
You sick lover enticing my heart,
Stealing my eyes from the world.

I hate you, you beast,
You know what you do.
I just want to love you,
To hold you, to kiss you.

Mature

Can we stop all the teasing,
And biting our lips.
The hugging our figures,
And shaking our hips.
The who slept with who,
the kisses we let slip.
I just want to be a kid a little longer.

Can we stop choosing partners,
Houses, jobs and pets.
Arguing over wedding outfits,
Or colour scheme bets.
Let's not retire in Paris,
Or worry about our debts.
I just want to be a kid a little longer.

Can we stop talking future,
And live in the moment.
Don't throw away childhoods,
Maturity's dangers - never content.
Stop drowning your sorrows,
Fill your heart with addictive torment.
I just want to be a kid a little longer.

Petrichor

The first crisp breath of the morning air,
So humid and breathable.
On a weekend,
you hear the mourning dove,
Telling you the day could never fail you.

The grass a little wet,
Almost as wet as the air seemed.
But that's okay,
It smells fresh.
Fog moving in to carry you away,
To whatever adventure the day would bring.

The sun brighter,
And beaming down.
The paddling pool getting blown up,
As you made your steady way to school.
Ready for when you return home,
Picky bits and ice pops for dinner.

This memory of childhood,
Although maybe it's us.
Who notice there's not as many stars in the night sky,
Because we never took a moment to look up.
We're asking where did the sound of mourning dove go,
Yet we never go outside to find it.

Can I go to the bathroom?

I walk down the old hall,
Not to use the bathroom,
But to get the look at myself,
That I've been dying to sneak.

To stare at my back that arches more than my ass,
Count the spots and rashes that flower on my face.
The bathroom is a place for judgement,
Why else would there be mirrors?

If not to look at my poor box frame,
Or my greasy hair that I swear washed a thousand times.
To listen to the girls gossip whilst putting on their pretty faces,
The boys ranking them from most to least 'fuckable'.

To fix my shirt to be more curvy around my hips and chest,
Walk back down the corridor with false confidence.
Return to class in hopes i've had a glow up on my way,
Want the world to stop the moment I walk through the door,
The cracked, ugly and fragile door.

Beginnings and ends

I miss you my love,
You've been gone so long.
I don't know how I can cope without you,
It feels like you're still here.

God knows how long I've been distant from your touch,
The touch I'll never feel again.
The rhythm of your heartbeat,
I'm starved of your attention.

My angel, my fallen,
My heaven no longer on earth.
Stars are jealous of your shine,
The moon cries for your looks.
So long you've been gone,
I miss you my love.

The unfortunate path

Life can be a series of unfortunate events,
One after the other, with no time for respite.
The life we live and crave is too alone,
With doves in one and tragedy in another.
We search for happiness, but it seems to elude us,
As if it's a mirage, always just out of reach.
We skim the clouds for faces of old,
Familiarity is always a welcomed sight.
But sometimes, the clouds obscure our view,
And we're left feeling lost and alone.

Porcelain memories

Porcelain dolls, so delicate and fine,
Their faces frozen in time,
Each one unique, yet all the same,
A beauty that can never fade.
Their beauty drawn on, and taken inspiration from,
but never spoilt of life.

Their beauty is eternal,
Their faces painted with care,
Inspiring awe and wonder,
For all who stop and stare.

Porcelain dolls,
 ones who've modelled their names.
 Through a glass window,
 a companion of remembrance.

Their names, forgotten by most,
But to us, they are still dear,
Memories of childhood,
And a time with no fear.

So let us cherish these dolls,
And the memories they hold,
For they are more than just toys,
They are treasures to behold.

Angels lullaby

The sleep we share with flourishing dreams, the giggling late at night.
The warmth of the covers and the soft, soothing light.

Stars call your name as you drift away to the sky,
sinking down to earth again like you did when you fell, my angel.

I'm grateful to be the one to watch over you, to make sure you're safe and sound.
You're my angel, my love, my everything.

As we drift off to sleep,
I'm comforted by the thought of waking up to another day with you,
my love. Sweet dreams.

Fluttering

Butterflies, so light and free,
A symbol of transformation,
From caterpillar to beauty,
A journey of creation.

Their wings, a canvas of colour,
A work of art, so fine,
Fluttering in the breeze,
A dance that's so divine.

They bring joy to all who see,
A reminder of hope and change,
That life is full of beauty,
And nothing stays the same.

So let the butterflies inspire,
And lift your spirits high,
For they are nature's masterpiece,
And a wonder to the eye.

Blade

Mascara running down my cheeks,
Sat on the foot of the bed.
I covered my closed eyes with my hands,
And thought back to the last thing you said.

You cried to me that you were trapped,
Whilst showing no emotion at all.
You felt weirdly empty that day,
Your ego ran rather small.

You blinked 10 times in our 3 minute talk,
Corrected me more than one.
Your glint still stealing the show in your eyes,
Yet the you that is you was all gone.

You laughed your laugh no times at all,
You smiled your smile to the floor.
Is it me that wet my cheeks to soon,
Or is it true that you are no more.

Midnight

Do I play on your mind at night,
Like a gentle lullaby.
Or maybe when you clear your thoughts,
Our future fills in the blanks.

When you gaze into the stars,
Is all you can see my eyes?
To think of home for you,
Would be to cup my body with yours.

Or even more so,
when you cry,
Does it feel worth it, to have my heart?
Do you stay up thinking 'Oh, how long now - 'til my woes make peace
with me'.

You find me in your dreams,
I assume,
In every stranger's face.
Or perhaps I'm simply delusional,
Finding myself in every mistaken place.

The dog who sits on the stairs

The dog who sits on the stairs,
He's been there for years and years.
Each car passes by,
He lets out a cry,
The dog who sits on the stairs.

Please let out not a peep,
For the dog, his job is to weep.
He waits and he waits,
For the sound of the gate,
The dog who sits on the stairs.

He hopes for you to come back,
With a cuddle and with a snack.
Listens out for the door,
Whilst he lays on the floor,
The dog who sits on the stairs.

The dog has fallen asleep,
After counting a number of sheep.
He dreams that your here,
Lets out his last tear,
The dog who sat on the stairs.

I don't see me here

If I wasn't born,
Would they die ever so softly,
Would the birds sing any more sweetly,
Would his heart still beat as willfully?

Would his soul pair to another,
And perhaps he's a little more happy.
Would he know that he missed me,
Can something that was never there be missing?

Would the air be as polluted,
Would my friends just simply replace me,
Would I know I should've been there,
And forever regret that I wasn't.

Do I question if I was here,
As surely it's all the same,
That if I was never there,
Nor were any of you.

Lost and found

When I was three,
I saw the city,
And left him behind,
Mr. Teddy,
My cuddly best buddy.

At age seven,
I went to a zoo,
So distracted,
By the giraffes long necks,
That I gave them my favourite toy by accident.

At twelve,
I thought I'd be killed,
As I'd lost my first ever phone,
I remember it being somewhere grassy?
Thankful that after 8 months,
Mum and dad gave in.

Only seventeen,
Sweet seventeen,
I found my most pure aspect,
And gave it away for promises.
I lost that boyfriend,
"I'm too young to be a dad!"
Still I had hope,
Hence your name.

18,
I became an adult.
Losing so much throughout my childhood,
Wishing for everything back,
I'd lost my childhood itself.

I didn't think to treasure the things I had,
until I lost them.
I didn't think you wouldn't get to lose them,
Until I lost you.

Haunting

Without you for too long,
And I don't know where I've held it.
Each time the sky disappears,
I drown myself in the scent you left on your side of our bed.

I can tell when heavens sour,
As you take it out on me.
Tormenting my rest and carrying the pain,
Until I see the moon again.

I can feel when you're close to me,
Carry me high to your cloud.
When you gift me with the kindest dreams,
There's no doubt that you're restful.

An angel like a moonlit river,
Where the stars in the reflection whisper your name.
And I forget you're even gone,
Until I see my moon again.

Ache

As doves fly with only peace,
you do so with beauty.
I wish to plaster the walls of my head,
with art created by your voice.
To drown myself in a bath of your laugh.

Tomorrow always seems too far,
Knowing you'll still not be mine.
I hug my pillow tight to my chest,
And I wish this all to go.
You steal my eyes from the world,
and you take my breath away with them.

I love you,
in a way that wakes me up in the morning.
I love you,
in a way I'd feel comfortable crying to.
I love you,
as who couldn't,
when you are truly you.

The lone land

The island calls for a friend,
Its surroundings want to surrender.
The ocean crashing its body,
Punching it's cliffs,
And stealing its rubble.
All it wants is a companion,
One that shares grass just as green,
And roots to its emotions,
Longing to be seen.
The island calls for a friend,
A familiar family,
An understanding horizon.
A safe for its love and affection,
The island calls for a friend.

Night culture

I can see the hollow line of my little town,
Lit by lamps over a brick built hill
Mellow and cold is the night
As it bites me as a Mercury woman.

My thoughts as plentiful as
The burning stars in the abyss,
They set alight the way home.
Headphones on,
And the world blocked out
I've never felt more unsafe.

Where the men lay
I do not know
For when I look over my shoulder
Searching for the camouflaged head
I see nothing
I fear everything.

Knowing every slowing car
Away to the green I go,
Far from the sense of eyes on me
Further from the witness of the glow.

I startle easy as my music swaps,
To a shallow thoughtless fear
I swear by the something
I heard in its absence
Walking at night all alone.

Out

Asleep on the plastic bay,
Desolate in surroundings and mind.
Where I'll go to I'm unsure,
Where I am now, I am blind.

Riding along the gusts of wind,
Speaking slowly to the trees.
I step over a puddle of brown,
And in it drops my keys.

My blurred home now left alone,
More so than me.
But I trust its eye,
For as long as it can see.

Cushions soften my fall,
The shoe box pixelation.
I'm hungry for company,
In my caravan situation.

My dad

I search every fathers day,
For something you don't know.
A line I haven't recited before,
One I could make sure doesn't seem rehearsed.
I tell you every fathers day,
How one in a million you are.
That I wish I could pay you back,
Or could just make it up to you.

Although I prove terrible,
For practising what a preach.
I promise you dad,
That you are my main man -
And I am your little girl.
Even though we change,
And maybe now i'm more a woman,
Or perhaps something else entirely,
You're still my knight in rusting armour.

I could write so much,
About how I've locked my heart.
I can talk about how painful it is.
How its been in for repair,
More times than I can count.
But I've never once mentioned,
The strict protector,
Picking up the pieces along the way.

Heaven in your voice

I was inspired,
When I met the man from the square,
His voice a work of art,
True music floods the air.
I ran and ran for plenty days,
Just waiting to once be struck,
In a perfect sudden I got hit down,
Unsure if it was mistress luck.

His voice painted the stars,
His words growing more in thought,
He was but a humble man,
Whose loud voice cleared the court.
I wanted to hear him,
Over and over,
I needed to hear him,
For he was my ears' lover.

Up and down the stairs I went,
Practically like a falcon would,
Preying on a CD player,
Wrecking everything I could.
Oh how I felt so inhumane,
And like a child again,
Adrenaline rushing through me,
How ink flows through a pen.

I felt like god selected me,
Told me himself that this is gold,
To always keep it close to me,
And that I had been told.
Never could I tell you,
How special and divine,
I've felt since I heard an angel,
A man whose name is Quine.

One thing that I don't have to share,
Yet that's something I'm proud to do,
Well I got to hear this life changing voice,
Let me change your life for you.
For now whether I'm a messenger,
Or that star that he has pardoned,
I swear you'll never hear quite a voice,
As the one I heard in Covent garden.

To live forever

Is this not a bad idea?
Am I really wasting a tree?
For you the reader to enjoy,
My silly poetry.

I can rhyme much like a rapper,
Spit bars like Eminem.
But is it worth the pride,
dear reader,
Do you even care for them?

I give my time,
And give my heart,
My emotions all ran out.
Now humour me and tell me,
From this book a plant shall sprout.

Atleast its not a best seller,
Though I really cannot lie -
Would I want some fame and fortune,
For the humble chance to die.

About the author

There isn't much to say this time,
Apart from how far I think I've come.
Still those feelings of loss and hate,
But perhaps more peace and love.

I could write plenty of pages,
About what this means to me.
How it's such a dangerous escape,
And hopefully a pleasure for you to read.

Though I really never could tell you,
When these silly feelings may end.
Maybe in my third book,
My sixth, eighth or tenth.

As I filled this book with my mind,
With plenty of help from words -
I felt this funny feeling,
That I've finally been heard.

Heard by myself that is,
As I really do ignore.
But hey,
I think I'll dwell on my feelings,
Just a little more.

Printed in Great Britain
by Amazon

32495121R00046